MW01045775

MUMMIES

STEPHEN SLOAN

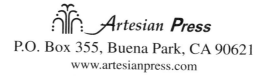

P.O. Box 355, Buena Park, CA 90621
www.artesianpress.com

Nonfiction
Ancient Egyptian Mystery Series

Cover photo courtesy of the Rosicrucian Egyptian Museum, San Jose, California
Project Editor: Molly Mraz
Illustrator: Fujiko
Graphic Design: Tony Amaro
©2004 Artesian Press

 *Artesian* **Press**

ISBN 1-58659-208-4

CONTENTS

Word List

Akh (ahk) The part of a person's soul that could live forever.

Ammit (AH-mitt) The god who could turn the Ka into a demon in the afterlife.

Anubis (uh-NOO-bihs) The god in charge of making mummies.

Ba (bah) The part of a person's soul that made that person different. It could go back to the land of the living to help people.

canopic jars (cuh-NAHP-ick) Jars that held the organs of the mummy.

hieroglyphs (HI-ruh-gliffs) Pictures that stood for words or sounds in the ancient Egyptian religious writing.

Horus (HOHR-uhs) The god of the land of the living.

Isis (I-sihs) A goddess and wife of Osiris.

jackal (JAK-uhl) A type of wild dog that hunts in packs at night.

Ka (kah) The part of a person's soul that would go to the land of the dead.

Ma'at (muh-AHT) The goddess of truth and pure deeds.

mummy (MUM-ee) A dead body that has been treated to keep it from decaying.

natron (NAY-trahn) A powder that dried the body of the mummy.

Osiris (oh-SI-rihs) The god of the land of the dead.

Pharaoh (FARE-oh) Another name for any of the kings who ruled ancient Egypt.

pyramid (PEER-uh-mid) A tomb that the ancient Egyptians built for the Pharaoh.

resin (REHZ-ihn) A liquid that turns to solid when it cools and was used in making mummies.

wabet (WAH-bit) The building near the tomb where a family brought a body. It was a clean place.

Chapter 1

The small room was dark. The only light came from the flashlight Howard held in his hand. There were many large boxes, several small boxes, jars, games, and pieces of furniture spread out on the floor. It looked as if somebody dropped them there long ago.

Howard pointed his flashlight at the wall. He saw beautiful picture writings. Howard was an expert in ancient Egyptian writing, so he understood what these pictures meant.

"These are magic writings and ancient prayers," he said out loud. But nobody could hear him. He was alone. Dust and dirt covered this small room,

Howard pointed his flashlight at the wall. He saw beautiful picture writings. Howard was an expert in ancient Egyptian writing, so he understood what the pictures meant.

which was deep underneath the sands of the Egyptian desert. Nobody had been in this room for 3,000 years.

The room was silent and still. The smell of old dust filled the cool air. Everything here remained untouched since the last human left the room so very long ago.

The only sound Howard heard was his own breathing. He wasn't scared, but he didn't exactly feel calm, either. He held the flashlight steady. His eyes were alert and ready in case anything moved. His body was tense. His open gun case hung from his waist.

Howard had walked through many curving hallways to get to this small underground room. Now he stood in the final death chamber of a wealthy businessman of ancient Egypt.

This rich man's name was Towag. When he was alive, he was a strong leader who wanted to make a lot of money. He had many slaves to work for him. If the slaves did not work hard enough, he beat them with whips and sticks. He did not give his slaves good food to eat. If they died, he did not care. He just bought more slaves and then used them until they died.

People were glad when Towag died. They wrote stories about him on the walls of the burial chamber. They made a mummy (MUM-ee) of his body and put it into a box. They put the box along the wall of the burial chamber. They also left things that the rich man used in his life. Then they left him there forever.

Howard was the only person who saw this room 3,000 years later. He did not want anybody else to get the credit or the fame for finding the treasures in the room, so he came alone.

The place was covered with dust. This burial chamber was untouched since the last ancient Egyptian closed the door.

There was not much air in the room. It was hard for Howard to breathe. He read the writing on the wall in a loud voice. He wasn't sure why he spoke out loud, since there was nobody there to hear him.

"This is the death chamber of Towag," the picture writing said. "Stop reading and leave now." Howard did not move. He was not afraid of words. He kept reading. A prayer for the dead man came next. Then there was a story from the man's life.

Near the box on the wall was a long row of picture writing. Howard started to read it. It was not like any Egyptian writing he had ever seen before. He shined his flashlight on the wall so he could see each word picture.

"Let this evil man stay here forever. Do not disturb his box. He was not good when he was alive. Let him stay here. Stop reading now and go away! The person who reads these words will wake Towag, and he will do terrible things."

Howard heard a noise. He turned quickly and moved his flashlight around the room. Nothing looked different. *Maybe it was a mouse,* he thought to himself. Then he realized that no mice could have been there for 3,000 years. He put his hand on his gun just to make sure it was there. He moved the flashlight back to the wall.

"Go away," said the picture writing. "If you stay here, you are in danger." Howard laughed and thought, *How could I be in danger from a man who is dead? There is nothing left of him. He is dust inside this box.*

Again, Howard heard a long scraping noise. He turned to shine his yellow light around the room. Everything still seemed the same. He thought, *Nothing moved even an inch.* Then the light shined on the box by the wall.

The brightly colored lid of the box was nearly halfway open. Howard knew that it was closed the last time he looked. He could not move. How did the box open? *Now* Howard was nervous. He moved the light to see if there was a rope or some kind of machine moving the lid. He saw nothing.

The lid continued to make a scraping sound as it slowly opened. In the light of the flashlight, Howard saw the right arm of the man inside. The arm was wrapped in old bandages. Some of them were hanging down in strips. The dirty bandages were yellow from age. As the lid opened, Howard could see more and more of the wrapped body. The body's right arm was pushing the lid open.

Howard saw the head of the dead body rise from the coffin. It was wrapped in the same kind of old bandages. The bandages on the head

As the lid opened, Howard could see more and more of the body. The body's right arm was pushing the lid open.

©2004 Fujiko

had two holes for eyes. Instead of eyes, two small fiery lights were shining through the dirty, torn bandages. Howard was so afraid, he could not move. He could not believe the mummy was really waking up.

Howard watched as the box's lid fell to the floor. The wrapped body was now free. Slowly the body sat up. The burning eyes looked straight ahead. Howard did not hear any noise now, but he heard words in his head. The words were not in any spoken language. Thoughts came into his mind. Howard knew that the thoughts were not his own. They were coming from the mummy.

Where am I? the thought asked. *What have they done to me for all these years?*

The body's right leg began to move up and reach out of the box. The body moved back and forth. Then it fell forward. The left leg swung out in front of the body. The mummy's thoughts entered Howard's mind: *Now I can walk.* Then the mummy became angry because he realized he was not alone.

I don't want anybody here! The head of Towag's mummy turned to look at the whole room. It looked right at Howard. Howard could see the fiery eyes get even brighter. He could almost feel their fire. Howard reached for his gun. He took one step back as he drew the weapon.

The mummy turned toward Howard and took a small step forward.

"Stop where you are!" Howard yelled. Whether or not the mummy could hear or understand these words, Howard would never know. The next step it took toward Howard was longer and stronger.

"Stop or I'll shoot!" he yelled. But then the m u m m y took another step closer. Howard had to act. His hands were shaking so much! His eyes were huge from fear.

The mummy turned toward Howard and took a step forward.

He pulled the trigger twice. The bullets hit the mummy's chest—right in the heart. But the mummy took another step toward Howard.

The mummy's thought entered Howard's head: *You can't kill the already dead.*

Howard took a step back and fell over a jar on the floor. The mummy's brain was in the jar. Howard was flat on his back on the floor when the mummy reached him.

When Howard did not return to his hotel that night, his friends were very worried. The next day, they went to the place where they thought Howard was working. They found the same entrance that Howard used and followed the hallways. They, too, found the death chamber.

They found Howard lying on the floor. He was dead. His face was blue and his eyes were wide open. He looked as though something horrible scared him to death. Everything else in the room looked untouched. Only one box was open. Its lid was on the floor. The box was empty. Towag was gone from his tomb.

• • • • • •

This is just a story.

It never happened.

It never could have happened in the real world. But is any of it true? Some parts of the story did happen in ancient Egypt many years ago. Some things are fake just to make it a good story.

It is true that some people who lived in ancient Egypt had their bodies turned into mummies. But why did people want to become mummies? And how were mummies made so long ago without modern science and equipment?

Chapter 2

Most people want to remember their loved ones after they die. Photographs help people remember what their loved ones looked like. Movie stars, singers, and important leaders are usually remembered, too. Retelling stories about people who are dead also keeps their memory alive. These stories can sometimes be good examples of how to live a good life or how to act in times of trouble or sadness. People sometimes want to act the same way a good person acted in life.

People in ancient Egypt were much like we are today. They wanted to remember important people and the things they did. Their religion helped them to remember, too.

There were no cameras to take pictures 3,000 years ago. There were no printing presses to make books about leaders and other famous people. That is one reason why the people in ancient Egypt kept the actual bodies of these people. They wrote and painted about their lives on the walls of burial chambers that were underground or inside special buildings called pyramids (PEER-uh-mids).

The people of ancient Egypt did not believe that death was the end of a life. They thought there was another beautiful life, called the afterlife, after they died. To live well in that next life, they needed to have some of the things that made them happy while they lived.

The place where dead people went to live again looked the same as the land of Egypt. When the soul of the dead person arrived in the new place, the soul would look for the things that made it happy before its death. The soul wanted its favorite food, nice furniture, favorite games, and its body.

There were two worlds in the religion of ancient Egypt—a land of the living and a land of the dead. Living people could not go to the land of the afterlife. Only the souls of dead people could travel to the land of the dead.

The reason the ancient Egyptians believed in a land of the living and a land of the dead was because of a story that was told as part of their religion. They believed that a god named Osiris (oh-SI-rihs) once ruled Egypt with his wife, Isis (I-sihs). Another god, Seth, became very jealous of them. He killed Osiris and cut his body into fourteen pieces. Isis found the pieces of Osiris's body and put them back together. When she did this, Osiris returned to life as a different god. The ancient Egyptians believed Osiris was a god who ruled over the land of the dead.

Osiris and Isis had a son named Horus (HOHR-uhs). Seth was still jealous and tried very hard to destroy Horus, just as he had tried to destroy Osiris. Horus and Seth battled many times until Horus finally won. When he did win, Horus became the god of the land of the living. That is why the ancient Egyptians believed Osiris ruled the land of the dead and his son Horus ruled the land of the living.

©Egyptian Museum, Cairo, Egypt

These are statues of Osiris (left), Isis (middle), and Horus (right).

People believed that the two lands were close to each other. The living believed that the dead could help them with their problems. The living wrote letters to dead people and put the letters in the death chambers. The letters asked for help and advice with everyday problems.

"Dear friend," someone wrote, "where is the best place to build my new house?"

The living people believed that their dead friends and family members would read the letters and then help them. They left food for their souls. They hoped that the dead people would come from the land of the dead, visit the death chamber, read the letters, and take the food.

The world of the living had many gods. The sun, moon, and stars were gods. The different kinds of weather were gods. Kings, called Pharaohs (FARE-ohs), were believed to be gods.

Some gods were pictured as humans with the heads of animals. Others were shown as animals with the heads of humans.

Some gods could change into different animals to help themselves and were shown as different animals. Some of the gods were men and some were women.

Anubis (uh-NOO-bihs) was the god in charge of what to do after a person died. He made the rules for making mummies and told the story of what happens to a person after death. Anubis was pictured as a human with the head of a jackal (JACK-uhl). Jackals are like wild dogs. They live in Africa and eat dead or dying animals.

When someone died, the Egyptians thought that the person's soul left the body. The soul then waited until the body was changed into a mummy before it began its journey to the afterlife.

The soul of a person had three parts. The first part was called the Ba (bah). It was what made a living person different from other living people. This part of the soul could come back to the world of the living and help its family and friends. The Ba was drawn as a bird with a human head.

The Akh (ahk) was the part of the soul that lived on and on. If the Akh was remembered, the person would never die.

The third part of the soul was the Ka (kah). The Ka was the part that would take the journey to the land of the dead, which was ruled by Osiris. The Ka had to pass many tests before the person could enter the land of the dead and live there forever.

The journey began after the person's body was turned into a mummy and put into the burial chamber. Part of the journey was a test of knowledge and a contest.

The Ka had to know the answers to many questions. Bad gods and demons wanted to stop the soul from getting to the afterlife. Some of the questions that the Ka had to answer were about the names of the gods, animals, and demons. The answers to the questions were painted on the walls of the burial chamber.

A special book called the *Book of the Dead* had many answers. This book was read to the dead person while the body was being turned into a mummy.

The final test came to the Ka in the Hall of Two Truths. Forty-two gods watched the final test in this great hall outside the entrance to the land of the dead.

The Ka entered the hall wearing its finest clothes. Its head was bowed. The god Anubis brought the Ka into the hall. The Ka went to Osiris and Isis. Between the gods and the Ka was a large balance scale. There was one feather from the bird goddess Ma'at (muh-AHT) in a dish on one side of the balance. Ma'at was the goddess of truth and pure deeds.

The dead person's heart was put in a dish on the other side of the scale. The heart was balanced against the one feather from Ma'at. If the person had done bad things in life, the heart would be heavy. A heavy heart pulled the balance down.

The feather was light. Even a few bad deeds pulled the heart down. A person had to be good all life long to keep the balance up. All the gods watched as the heart told them whether the person was going to be allowed to enter the land of the dead or whether the worst thing would happen. If the feather pulled up and the heart pulled down, Ammit (AH-mitt) came.

Ammit had the head of a crocodile, the front of a lion, and the back end of a hippopotamus. Ammit would eat the heart, and the Ka would never enter the land of the dead. It would become a demon.

If the heart did not pull the balance down, the gods gave the Ka food and drink. The Ka could then enter the land of the dead. There were many staircases and doors painted in the burial chamber, so that the Ka could get out of the pyramid.

Only one thing could spoil life in the land of the dead. The dead person could not be forgotten. The family had to remember him or her forever. The family members could bring food to the burial place to show that they remembered. They could write the name of the person. They could talk about the person.

If a soul was forgotten, it stopped living in the land of the dead. The Ba, Ka, and Akh ended. If the mummy was destroyed, there was no place for the soul to go. Then the soul in the land of the dead no longer lived. Both the mummy and the memory of a person had to be maintained.

Chapter 3

Long before someone died, the family picked out a burial place. Much thought and work went into choosing this place. Great Pharaohs built large pyramids that took many years to complete. Others built underground tombs. Some underground tombs were hidden for thousands of years and are just now being found.

The family made a sad trip across the Nile River when one of its members died. The family brought the body to a building near the tombs of the dead. The building was called a wabet (WAH-bit), or clean place.

A priest was in charge at the wabet. Everything that the priest and his workers did was written in the *Book of the Dead*. The *Book of the Dead* was a book of instructions and prayers. The prayers often used the name of the person who was dead. The person's name was written in the book. Each person had his or her own book. There were no printing presses, so each book was written by hand in the picture writing of the Egyptians called hieroglyphs (HI-ruh-gliffs). The *Book of the Dead* was placed inside the tomb of each person.

Special workers were chosen to work in the wabet. The priests lived outside of the city. They usually lived on the west side of the Nile River, near the tombs.

The god of the making of mummies was Anubis. The priest wore a mask of Anubis as he read from the *Book of the Dead*. He read the prayers, and the workers followed his instructions.

First, the body was washed and all

of the blood was drained out of it. Then a cut was made on the left side. The cut started below the ribs and went down. The hole was big enough for workers to remove some of the internal organs. Not all of the organs had to come out.

When the organs were taken out, they were put into special containers called canopic (cuh-NAHP-ick) jars. The jars were made of a beautiful white stone called alabaster. The stone jars had prayers written on the front.

Each jar was a symbol for one of the sons of Horus, and each held a special part of the body. The different sons of Horus were shown as a falcon, a baboon, a jackal, and a man. When a jar was closed, it was supposed to stay closed forever.

The falcon jar held the intestines. The baboon jar held the lungs. The jackal jar held the stomach. The human jar held the liver of the dead person.

Canopic jars held the organs of a mummy.

When the workers finished taking out the organs, they took out the brain. The workers started with the left nostril of the nose. They put a metal rod up the nostril and broke a small bone inside the head. They used tools to pull the brain out through the nose. They did not have to break any of the skull bones, so the head looked normal.

To make sure that the head kept its shape, the workers filled the empty skull with resin (REHZ-ihn). Resin is like plastic. It is liquid when it is hot. When it cools, it becomes solid. The solid resin helped the head of the body keep its normal shape. The resin was poured into the head through the same hole that the workers used to take out the brain.

Some body organs were not kept or saved for the afterlife. They were thrown away. One of the organs that was left inside the body was the heart. The heart was important for the trial of goodness. The Egyptians believed that the heart was where thoughts and feelings came from.

When the body was empty and the jars were filled, the workers dried the body. They rubbed it with natron (NAY-trahn). Natron is a powder made of chemicals. One of these chemicals was salt. It is the same kind of salt that is put on food.

The workers rubbed natron on the outside and the inside of the body. Natron dried the body. It took more than two months to dry completely.

The body was almost flat when it was dry. Most of the insides had been taken out. To return the body to its normal shape, the workers put linen cloth inside. Sometimes they used straw. They tried to make the body look natural, the way it did when it was alive.

After the body was stuffed, the workers washed it with water from the Nile River. Then they rubbed the dead body with sweet-smelling oils. While they worked, the priest said prayers from the *Book of the Dead.* Some of the prayers told the soul what to do on the way to the land of the dead.

Next, the workers put the body on the lion table. The lion table was shaped like a standing lion. It had the face of a lion. The legs of the table looked like the legs of a lion. The back of the lion was flat, so that it could support the body. The lion table was usually made of wood.

As the priest said more prayers, the workers covered the body with tar and resin. Tar is a black, sticky oil. The tar and resin kept air from touching the skin. Air carries germs that can hurt the skin. The tar and resin made the skin turn dark.

Next, the body was wrapped with linen cloth. Linen is the kind of cloth used to make sheets. Rich people bought brand-new linen for the mummy. Poor people brought their old cloth for the priests to use. The linen was cut into strips like bandages.

Every part of the body was covered in strips of linen. The workers started with the fingers and toes of the body. They wrapped carefully. Each finger and each toe was wrapped separately. Sometimes a gold tag was put on the big toe of the mummy before it was wrapped in linen.

After the fingers and toes were wrapped, the feet and legs came next. Small gold medals and small stone statues were wrapped inside the linen bandages. Rich people had more gold in their mummies than poor people. The gold and small statues made the mummies very valuable.

The mummy's arms were wrapped and crossed over the chest. This was the way Osiris was pictured. The mummy's arms were put in the same position, so that it would be ready for the afterlife.

As the priest said prayers, the workers covered each layer of linen bandages with resin to protect it from the air. Before the head was finished, the priest put a mask over the mummy's face. Records from early Egyptian

Photograph courtesy of the Rosicrucian Egyptian Museum, San Jose, CA

The mummy's arms were crossed over the chest.

history show that the priest painted a face on the bandages. Later the mummies of important people were given very fancy masks. A great Pharaoh might have a large golden mask.

The last step was to cover the whole body in a layer of linen bandages. Then the body was put into a wooden box called the coffin.

In earlier times, the inner coffins were shaped like boxes. Later, the boxes were made more in the shape of a human body. The inner coffin was the first of many boxes that would hold the mummy. The outside of the inner coffin was painted with the name of the mummy, many prayers, and some painted eyes so the mummy could "see" outside the coffin.

It took about seventy days from when the body came to the wabet until the mummy was ready. The family of the dead person could then take the mummy away. When the priest gave the mummy to the family, he also gave them a copy of the *Book of the Dead*.

The family of the dead person was then ready to take the mummy to its final resting place.

Chapter 4

It was time for the soul to make the long journey into another world.

The last ceremony for the body was at the place of burial. A Pharaoh or a rich person had a very big ceremony. Today this ceremony is called a funeral. A poor person had a smaller funeral.

The mummy of a Pharaoh or rich person was carried from the east side of the Nile River. The mummy was in its inner coffin. There was a parade. The mummy was followed by priests, family members, female dancers, friends, and other people. They rode in a boat to the west side of the Nile River and then walked to the burial place. The parade was met by more priests and some male dancers. The priests sang songs and said prayers. The dancers danced to honor the person who had died. Then they carried the mummy to the tomb.

A tomb is where a body is placed. The size of the tomb depended on how much money the family had. A Pharaoh could build a large pyramid for his tomb. For a poor man or woman, a hole in the sand was his or her tomb. People with money built tombs underground to hold the mummies of their entire family.

A tomb had at least two rooms. The smaller room contained the mummy. This room was called the burial chamber. The larger room was filled with things that the dead person loved in life.

The tomb was a beautiful place. The walls were painted with bright colors. They were covered with picture writing. The walls told stories. They had prayers and pictures of gods. They showed life in Egypt. They showed the life of the person who was buried in the tomb.

The last ceremony took place just before the mummy was put into the burial chamber. It was called the Opening of the Mouth. However, the priest did not really open the mouth of the mummy.

The open coffin with the mummy inside was stood up against a wall. Then the priest touched the outside of the mummy where the mouth should be. This was the symbol of making the mouth come alive. Then the priest rubbed the mummy's face with milk.

The priest hugged the mummy. This showed that the mummy was leaving the land of the living and that the family would remember the person forever. Then the coffin with the mummy was put into the outer coffins.

Usually there were three coffins: the

inner one with the mummy inside and two outer coffins. The last coffin was made of strong stone or heavy wood. Each coffin was painted with words, prayers, and pictures. Eyes and doors were painted on the coffins so that the mummy could "see" outside, and the soul of the person could use the doors to get out.

A shrine was built around the three coffins. Family members and friends of the dead person could put flowers or gifts into the shrine before the priest closed the doors and tied them with rope. The ends of the rope were covered with clay, and the priest used a seal to show who was inside the shrine. The shrine and seal were never to be opened.

Then it was time to end the ceremony for the dead. A feast of beef and a bull's heart was left near the shrine for the dead person. The canopic jars, which held the lungs, liver, stomach, and intestines, were also left near the shrine. The priest left linen cloth for the mummy to wear in the land of the dead.

When everything that the mummy needed was placed in the small room, the people left. The entry was closed with bricks and cement so that no one could enter.

It was very important that the mummy be left alone and not be hurt. The soul of the person could not live in the afterlife if the mummy was not whole. The pictures of gods were there to protect the mummy from bad spirits. The bricked-up door was closed to protect the mummy from bad people.

The large room was filled with things that the living person liked. The pictures on the wall told stories of what the person had done while alive. It showed events that should be remembered.

There were many things in the tomb

that were necessary for the mummy to use in the afterlife. Not all of them were for the soul. Things that the living person liked were put into the tomb. If the person had liked to hunt, spears and arrows were put into the room. If the person had liked to ride horses or drive wagons, a whole wagon was put in with the mummy.

Hair combs and face cream were left. Games and toys that the person liked were left, too. A king or queen might have a favorite chair or special clothes put into the rooms. Many of their items were made of gold and priceless stones.

Animals that were pets of the Pharaoh were also made into mummies and put into the tomb. The animals could go with the mummy into the afterlife.

Statues of servants were put into the tomb. If the living person had ten servants, then ten statues of servants

Photograph courtesy the Rosicrucian Egyptian Museum, San Jose, CA

This board game, called Senet, was left in a tomb. It was very popular with ancient Egyptians. Everyone, from the Pharaoh to servants, played this game from childhood.

were put into the tomb. Statues of the living person were put into the tomb, too, so that if anything happened to the mummy, the soul could find a place to stay.

The last part of the funeral was a meal. The family ate a meal in the large room, but they did not clean up after they were done. They left the food and dishes in the tomb. This showed the soul that life was not finished, just as the meal was not finished.

At last the ceremony ended. Everybody stood up to leave and then walked out of the tomb. All was silent. Nothing of life was left inside.

Bricks were put over the door of the tomb. The mummy, all of the contents of the rooms, and all of the pictures of the gods became dark and quiet. A seal was put on the outside of the tomb with the name of the person who was inside.

Guards stood outside to be sure that nobody would disturb the tomb. Grave robbers might want to break in and steal all the gold and gifts inside the tomb. Guards had to be paid to protect the tombs.

Paying guards did not always work. Many of the tombs of the ancient Egyptians were robbed. The robberies took place soon after the person was put into the tomb. The robbers took the gold and valuable items from the tomb. Sometimes the robbers opened the coffins and disturbed the mummies, looking for the gold wrapped in the bandages of the mummy.

In the thousands of years since the building of the tombs, many people have wondered about them. Scientists have opened the tombs to study them. They wanted to learn about how the mummies were made. Historians wanted to learn how to read the picture writing. They were also interested in the life and religion of the people of ancient Egypt. To learn about these things meant doing the one thing that the people who made the mummies didn't want: The mummies had to be disturbed.

Chapter 5

Egyptians were not the only ones who kept bodies. Whenever a body is kept and made to look like it did originally, it is a mummy.

Some mummies were made by nature, some by accident, and some by hard work. The oldest mummy was not a person. It was the body of an animal that is no longer living on the earth. It was the frozen body of a mammoth.

The mammoth was a large animal that looked like an elephant. Mammoths lived after the dinosaurs but before modern humans. They were bigger than elephants and were covered with long hair.

Scientists found mummies of mammoths in Siberia. This picture shows what a mammoth looked like.

Many thousands of years ago, the earth turned cold, and ice began to cover the northern parts of the world. The ice and cold took the animals by surprise. The temperature got very cold very fast. The animals died. Ice covered the bodies of some of the animals––just as if they were put into a freezer. The frozen mammoths were in the ice for many, many years. In the northern part of Russia, called Siberia, several people found frozen mammoths.

At first, no one believed these stories. Then scientists went there and saw the large bodies.

The scientists did not know what kind of animals were frozen. They knew that they were not modern elephants. After studying the animals, scientists learned that the frozen, elephant-like animals lived about 20,000 years ago.

In 1991, two people were hiking near a trail in the high mountains near the borders of Switzerland and Austria. They saw something in the snow. When they went closer, they saw that it was a person. But the person had not fallen that day. The hikers went to a hotel to call the police. When the police arrived at the mountain, they saw that the body was frozen in the ice. Its clothes were not from this time. They called scientists to look at the body. The scientists studied it. They were surprised to find that it was a man who lived more than 4,000 years ago.

Scientists found seeds in his clothes, telling them that it was autumn when he died. He wore clothes made of animal fur. He had gloves with him. His gloves were made of tree bark. They were stuffed with dry grass to keep his hands warm. Dry grass was also in his shoes. His shoes were tied to his feet with strips of animal skin.

The "Ice Man" had a knife made of stone. He carried his knife in a cover made of tree bark that was tied together with strips of grass. He carried an ax with a wooden handle and a blade made of copper. He had a backpack on a frame made of wood. He had some tools to make a bow, and a bow that was not finished.

Scientists thought that his job was to take care of sheep. He probably was taking the sheep down from the mountains before winter. Scientists guessed that along the way, he fell off the path and down the mountain. He hit his head on the rocks and died.

Everything he was carrying fell with him. His body became frozen. Then snow and ice covered him. The cold climate kept most of his body unchanged. Four thousand years later, the climate grew warmer in that part of the world. The ice began to melt. That's when the hikers found his body.

In the year 2001, scientists made an important discovery while studying the "Ice Man." They found an arrow tip in a bone in his back. This was important because it changed what scientists had first thought. At first, they thought the ice man died from a terrible fall. However, the arrow tip found in his

A scientist examines the mummy of the "Ice Man."

back could mean that someone shot him with the arrow first and then he fell. If that is true, it could be the earliest known murder ever committed. The world may never know.

Many years ago, the people who lived above the Arctic Circle, near the cold North Pole, placed dead people in the frozen ground. They knew that cold would keep the bodies for many years. They put objects from the dead people's lives in the ground with them. These mummies have lasted for many years. They are even older than the mummies in the tombs of Egypt.

In South America, the Inca Indians made mummies of important people. The bodies of the ancients were dried by the sands of the desert. The bodies were wrapped and placed at the bottom of deep holes dug in the sand. They were placed in a circle facing out. They were sitting up. Faces were painted on the wrappings. The bodies looked like they were ready to talk to the living people who came to visit them.

Recent discoveries in China have uncovered mummies there. Some mummies of light-haired Western people were naturally mummified. Also, important people from the Han Dynasty of around 100 B.C. to 100 A.D. were mummified by people with special knowledge.

The ground itself can be a way to save the bodies of dead people. In England, Ireland, and many other places, there is an unusual kind of dirt called peat. Peat is made from old plants and chemicals. People who cut the peat out of the earth have found human bodies.

The bodies were not treated in any way. The peat itself saved the bodies. No one is sure why they were put into the peat. It is possible that people were accidentally trapped and died there.

In a city in Mexico, the earth saved many of the bodies of people who were buried there. No one knew that the earth in the cemetery was perfect for saving bodies. Bodies lasted for more than 100 years. The cemetery became full, and the people wanted to make room for more burials. They started to dig up some of the old graves. They were quite surprised to see that the bodies had become mummies.

Today, people visit a museum of mummies to see how the dirt in Mexico saved the bodies of the people who were buried there. The dirt kept all of the bodies in good condition, whether they were young or old, rich or poor.

Most people no longer believe the way the ancient Egyptians believed.

People may no longer believe in making mummies, but almost everyone wants to be remembered by their loved ones. It may not be too different from the ancients, who believed that as long as people are remembered, they will never leave the happy land of the dead.

Bibliography

Brier, Bob. *The Encyclopedia of Mummies.* New York: Facts on File, 1998.

Dunand, Françoise, and Roger Lichtenberg. *Mummies: A Voyage Through Eternity.* Philadelphia: Harry N. Abrams, 1994.

McHargue, Gorgess. *Mummies.* Philadelphia: Lippincott, 1972.

Reeves, Nicholas, with Nan Froman. *Into the Mummy's Tomb.* New York: Scholastic, 1992.

Spindler, Konrad. *The Man in the Ice.* New York: Harmony Books, 1994.

Time-Life Books. *What Life Was Like on the Banks of the Nile.* Alexandria, Va., 1996.

Tyldesley, Joyce. *The Mummy: Unwrap the Ancient Secrets of the Mummies' Tombs.* London: Carlton, 1999.

Watterson, Barbara. *The Gods of Ancient Egypt.* New York: Facts on File, 1984.

Artesian Press

High Interest...Easy Reading

Multicultural Read-Alongs

Standing Tall Mystery Series

Mystery chapter books that portray young ethnic Americans as they meet challenges, solve puzzles, and arrive at solutions. By doing the right thing the mystery falls away and they are revealed to have been...Standing Tall!

Set 1	Book	Cassette	CD
Don't Look Now or Ever	1-58659-084-7	1-58659-094-4	1-58659-266-1
Ghost Biker	1-58659-082-0	1-58659-092-8	1-58659-265-3
The Haunted Hound	1-58659-085-5	1-58659-095-2	1-58659-267-X
The Howling House	1-58659-083-9	1-58659-093-6	1-58659-269-6
The Twin	1-58659-081-2	1-58659-091-X	1-58659-268-8

Set 2			
As the Eagle Goes	1-58659-086-3	1-58659-096-0	1-58659-270-X
Beyond Glory	1-58659-087-1	1-58659-097-9	1-58659-271-8
Shadow on the Snow	1-58659-088-X	1-58659-098-7	1-58659-272-6
Terror on Tulip Lane	1-58659-089-8	1-58659-099-5	1-58659-273-4
The Vanished One	1-58659-100-2	1-58659-090-1	1-58659-274-2

Set 3			
Back From the Grave	1-58659-101-0	1-58659-106-1	1-58659-345-5
Guilt	1-58659-103-7	1-58659-108-8	1-58659-347-1
Treasure In the Keys	1-58659-102-9	1-58659-107.X	1-58659-346-3
"I Didn't Do It!"	1-58659-104-5	1-58659-109-6	1-58659-348-X
Of Home and Heart	1-58659-105-3	1-58659-110-X	1-58659-349-8

www.artesianpress.com

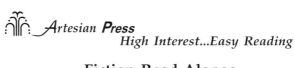

Artesian **Press**

High Interest...Easy Reading

Fiction Read-Alongs

Take 10 Books

Mystery	Books	Cassette	CD
Nobody Lives in Apartment N-2			
	1-58659-001-4	1-58659-006-5	1-58659-275-0
Return of the Eagle	1-58659-002-2	1-58659-007-3	1-58659-276-9
Touchdown	1-58659-003-0	1-58659-008-1	1-58659-277-7
Stick Like Glue	1-58659-004-9	1-58659-009-x	1-58659-278-5
Freeze Frame	1-58659-005-7	1-58659-010-3	1-58659-279-3
Adventure			
Cliffhanger	1-58659-011-1	1-58659-016-2	1-58659-280-7
The Great UFO Frame-Up			
	1-58659-012-x	1-58659-016-2	1-58659-281-5
Swamp Furies	1-58659-013-8	1-58659-018-9	1-58659-282-3
The Seal Killers	1-58659-014-6	1-58659-019-7	1-58659-283-1
Mean Waters	1-58659-015-4	1-58659-020-0	1-58659-284-x
Sports			
The Phantom Falcon	1-58659-031-6	1-58659-036-7	1-58659-290-4
Half and Half	1-58659-032-4	1-58659-037-5	1-58659-291-2
Knucklehead	1-58659-033-2	1-58659-038-3	1-58659-292-0
The Big Sundae	1-58659-034-0	1-58659-039-0	1-58659-293-9
Match Point	1-58659-035-9	1-58659-040-5	1-58659-294-7
Chillers			
Alien Encounter	1-58659-051-0	1-58659-056-1	1-58659-295-5
Ghost in the Desert	1-58659-052-9	1-58659-057-x	1-58659-296-3
The Huanted Beach House			
	1-58659-053-7	1-58659-058-8	1-58659-297-1
Trapped in the Sixties	1-58659-054-5	1-58659-059-6	1-58659-298-x
The Water Witch	1-58659-055-3	1-58659-060-x	1-58659-299-8
Thrillers			
Bronco Buster	1-58659-041-3	1-58659-046-4	1-58659-325-0
The Climb	1-58659-042-1	1-58659-047-2	1-58659-326-9
Search and Rescue	1-58659-043-x	1-58659-048-0	1-58659-327-7
Timber	1-58659-044-8	1-58659-048-0	1-58659-328-5
Tough Guy	1-58659-045-6	1-58659-050-2	1-58659-329-3
Fantasy			
The Cooler King	1-58659-061-8	1-58659-066-9	1-58659-330-7
Ken and the Samurai	1-58659-062-6	1-58659-067-7	1-58659-331-5
The Rabbit Tattoo	1-58659-063-4	1-58659-068-5	1-58659-332-2
Under the Waterfall	1-58659-064-2	1-58659-069-3	1-58659-333-1
Horror			
The Indian Hills Horror	1-58659-072-3	1-58659-077-4	1-58659-335-8
From the Eye of the Cat	1-58659-071-5	1-58659-076-6	1-58659-336-6
The Oak Tree Horror	1-58659-073-1	1-58659-078-2	1-58659-337-4
Return to Gallows Hill	1-58659-075-8	1-58659-080-4	1-58659-338-2
The Pack	1-58659-074-x	1-58659-079-0	1-58659-339-0
Romance			
Connie's Secret	1-58659-460-5	1-58659-915-1	1-58659-340-4
Crystal's Chance	1-58659-459-1	1-58659-917-8	1-58659-341-2
Bad Luck Boy	1-58659-458-3	1-58659-916-x	1-58659-342-0
A Summer Romance	1-58659-140-1	1-58659-918-6	1-58659-343-9
To Nicole With Love	1-58659-188-6	1-58659-919-4	1-58659-344-7

www.artesianpress.com

Other Nonfiction Read-Along

Disasters

- Challenger
- The Kuwaiti Oil Fires
- The Last Flight of 007
- The Mount St. Helens Volcano
- The Nuclear Disaster at Chernobyl

Disaster Display Set (5 each of 5 titles 25 books in all)
80106

Natural Disasters

- Blizzards
- Earthquakes
- Hurricanes and Floods
- Tornadoes
- Wildfires

Disaster Display Set (5 each of 5 titles 25 books in all)
80032